Magic, Myth, and Mystery

GHOSTS

DO YOU BELIEVE?

This series features creatures that excite our minds. They're magical. They're mythical. They're mysterious. They're also not real. They live in our stories. They're brought to life by our imaginations. Facts about these creatures are based on folklore, legends, and beliefs. We have a rich history of believing in the impossible. But these creatures only live in fantasies and dreams. Monsters do not live under our beds. They live in our heads!

45th Parallel Press

Published in the United States of America by Cherry Lake Publishing
Ann Arbor, Michigan
www.cherrylakepublishing.com

Reading Adviser: Marla Conn MS, Ed., Literacy specialist, Read-Ability, Inc.
Cover Design: Felicia Macheske

Photo Credits: © Bundit Yuwannasiri/Shutterstock.com, cover; © Sabphoto/Shutterstock.com, cover; © Olexandra/Shutterstock.com, 1; © Tom Tom/Shutterstock.com, 5; © DJTaylor/Shutterstock.com, 7; © Pikul Noorod/Shutterstock.com, 8; © MelBrackstone/Shutterstock.com, 11; © Ure/Shutterstock.com, 12; © Joe Prachatree/Shutterstock.com, 15; © eddtoro/ Shutterstock.com, 17; © Everett Collection/Shutterstock.com, 18; © Yezepchyk Oleksandr/Shutterstock.com, 21; © Anirut Thailand/Shutterstock.com, 22; © Nigel Jones/ Wikimedia Commons, 25; From The New York Public Library, 27; © Zack Frank/Shutterstock.com, 28

Graphic Elements Throughout: © denniro/Shutterstock.com; © Libellule/Shutterstock.com; © sociologas/ Shutterstock.com; © paprika/Shutterstock.com; © ilolab/Shutterstock.com; © Bruce Rolff/Shutterstock.com

45th Parallel Press is an imprint of Cherry Lake Publishing.

Library of Congress Cataloging-in-Publication Data has been filed and is available at catalog.loc.gov

Cherry Lake Publishing would like to acknowledge the work of The Partnership for 21st Century Skills.
Please visit *www.p21.org* for more information.

Printed in the United States of America
Corporate Graphics

TABLE of CONTENTS

Creepy Cold Spots

What are ghosts? What are different types of ghosts?

"Boo!" Many people report seeing ghosts. They see ghost people. They see ghost animals. They see ghost buildings. They see ghost ships. They report strange activities. They hear noises. They see strange lights. They feel cold air. These are signs of ghosts.

Living things die. The bodies rot. They become part of the earth. Some people believe **souls** still live. Souls are spirits. Most souls move on. They go to heaven or hell. But some souls get stuck on earth. These souls become ghosts. Ghosts are souls that can be seen by the living. There are different reasons for becoming ghosts. Some people have unfinished business. Some have died violently.

Ghosts are also called "spooks" or "phantoms."

Explained by Science!

People tend to see ghosts in old buildings. Scientists say they're not seeing ghosts. They're affected by mold. Old buildings may have mold. Mold creates poor air quality. It affects human brains. It may cause changes in mood. It may cause anger. It may make it hard to think. It may cause memory loss. It may cause fear. It may cause people to see things. People think they see ghosts. Shane Rogers is an engineering professor at Clarkson University. He explores haunted houses. He looks for mold. He said, "Many of the places under investigation and from my own experiences may be prime environments for mold and other indoor air quality issues."

Some people think ghosts are mind tricks.

Some people think ghosts are visitors from another time and place. They think there are different worlds. They think there are different timelines. Ghosts find **portals**. Portals are doorways. They cross portals. They enter our space.

Some people think ghosts are demons or angels. Demons hurt people. They trick people. Angels are **guardians**. Guardians protect people.

Some people think ghosts feed off energy. The world is made of energy. People are made of energy. Ghosts use this energy.

Ghosts interact with the living. They can be seen. They can be heard. They can be felt. They do things for attention. Some ghosts cause harm.

Ghosts can be **intelligent** or **residual**. Intelligent ghosts are smart. They know what they're doing. Residual ghosts are leftover from past events. They live their final hours over and over.

Ghosts don't look the same. Some are **invisible**. This means they can't be seen. Some look like white air. Some look human. There are many types of ghosts.

Crisis ghosts are one example. Crisis means emergency. These ghosts appear once. They show up when someone dies. They say good-bye. They give important information.

Vengeful ghosts are another example. Vengeful means they want to get even. They were wrongly killed. They seek to hurt those who hurt them.

Ghosts come in all shapes and sizes.

Chapter Two

Haunting Powers

What does it mean to haunt?
What powers do ghosts have?

Ghosts keep their personalities. If they were evil people, they're evil ghosts. If they were good people, they're good ghosts. Evil ghosts **haunt** the living. Haunt means to bother. Evil ghosts feed off bad energy. They feed off their **victims'** fear. Victims are people being haunted. Good ghosts protect the living. They don't cause harm.

Ghosts are **bound** to an object, person, or place. Bound means to be stuck with. They're trapped where they died. They haunt these places. They do this for a long time. They try to scare the living away. They haunt people. They may follow people around.

Ghosts can be anywhere.

Ghosts have many powers. They use these powers to haunt. They make sounds humans can't make. They **wail**. Wails are loud yells. Ghost wails are scary. They can also hurt people's ears.

Ghosts can change the air. They can make air really cold. They can make air really hot. They can fly. They can pass through walls. They're fast. They're strong. They can move from place to place. They can move things. They control electronics.

Some ghosts can make copies of themselves. They do this to confuse humans. Some ghosts can change shapes.

Some ghosts can control dreams. They talk to people in dreams. They give people nightmares. They steal energy from dreams.

Young children can see ghosts the best.

Chapter Three

Giving Up the Ghost

What is a major ghost weakness? What are ghost hunters? How can you get rid of ghosts?

Ghosts can't kill. This is their greatest weakness. But they use ghost powers. They mess with people. They drive people crazy. They scare them. They get people to endanger themselves. They get people to hurt others.

It's hard to get rid of ghosts. Ghosts have all the time in the world. They can haunt forever. So, people need help. They need to call ghost hunters. Ghost hunters find ghosts. They help people feel less scared. They try to understand ghosts. They try to understand hauntings. They find the source of the strange activity.

Ghosts depend on people's fear.

When Fantasy Meets Reality!

Scientists discovered a new animal. They named it Casper. Casper looks like Casper the friendly cartoon ghost. Casper is a deep-sea octopod. It's white. It's clear. It doesn't have any pigment. Pigment means color. It has two black eyes. Casper lives 13,000 feet (3,962 meters) below sea level. It lives near Hawaii. It looks like an octopus. It has eight arms. It lives a long time. It moves very slowly. It takes a long time to have babies. It lays few eggs. It lays its eggs on the seafloor. It lays its eggs on valuable earth metals. But deep ocean mining is causing harm. Companies want the metals to make high-tech things. Casper is at high risk for becoming a ghost.

Ghost hunters consider themselves to be scientists.

Ghost hunters help people feel safe. They investigate haunted places. They find proof. They study proof. They record details. They conduct tests. They look for clues. They interview many people. They ask many questions.

They use many tools. They use special cameras. These cameras take pictures in the dark. They study the pictures. They look for dark shadows. They look for glowing **mists**, or fogs. They look for **orbs**. Orbs are round balls of light. Some believe orbs are ghosts trying to be seen. They look for **vortexes**. Vortexes are swirling lights. They hunt down ghosts.

Ghost whisperers are a type of medium.

After finding ghosts, people need to get rid of them. There are different ways.

People can make sure spirits of the dead are at rest. Some families give gifts to their dead relatives. Some do ceremonies for the spirit. Some call for an **exorcism**. Exorcisms are special rituals. Religious people perform acts. They force ghosts out of people. They use holy words. They use holy water. They use holy tools.

Some people **summon** ghosts. Summon is to call. **Mediums** talk to ghosts. They call ghosts. They find out what's wrong. They try to solve problems. They tell ghosts to go away.

SURVIVAL TIPS!

- Yell at ghosts. Say out loud, "You may not follow me."

- Don't go ghost hunting alone. Go with others. Do this for safety. Do this for witnesses.

- Talk to ghosts. Tell them to leave.

- Use thermal equipment. Thermal detects heat. Heat is a form of energy. This is a way to make ghosts more visible.

- Get a cat. Wait for the cat to stare into space. This means a ghost is near. Animals can sense ghosts.

- Don't build on top of limestone or water. Limestone keeps energy. Water is an energy conductor. Ghosts like energy.

- Avoid dark shadows. Avoid glowing mists. Avoid round balls of light. Avoid swirling lights.

Chapter Four

Ghosts Around the Globe

How long have ghosts been around? What are ghosts from other cultures like?

Ghosts have been around since ancient times. Pliny the Younger was an ancient Roman author. He lived in the first century. He wrote about a ghost. He saw an old man with a long beard. The old man wore chains. He haunted Pliny's house.

Ancient Egyptians believed in ghosts. They believed souls lived after death. They built **pyramids**. These are special buildings. They were tombs for kings and queens. Ghosts lived there until they moved on to the next world.

Ancient Greeks hosted feasts. Feasts are great parties. These parties have lots of food. The Greeks honored spirits of the dead.

People have always wondered what happens after death.

Many different cultures believe in ghosts. In India, ghosts are *bhoot* or *aojha*. Bhoot are stuck. They're restless. They haunt people. Aojha are ghost guides.

Chinese people believe in hungry ghosts. Hungry ghosts have tiny throats. They have big stomachs. They can never be full. They visit their families. They visit their old homes. They feed off fear. Chinese people give hungry ghosts gifts. They give food. They give drinks. They give money. This keeps hungry ghosts away.

Confucius said, "Respect ghosts and gods, but keep away from them."

Know the Lingo!

- **Apparition:** the visible appearance of a ghost

- **Aura:** a field of energy

- **Child ghosts:** ghosts of children that are lonely and want attention; probably demons in disguise

- **Entity:** an interactive ghost

- **Going ghost:** having the power to change from human to ghost

- **Harbinger:** a ghost of the future that warns people of events

- **Hot spots:** areas where most activity is concentrated

- **Infestation:** haunting done by many ghosts

- **Poltergeist:** mischievous spirit, "noisy ghost"

- **Possession:** an evil ghost controlling a human body

- **Psychic:** having to do with a person's soul or mind

- **Séance:** a ritual to communicate with spirits of the dead

- **Specter:** apparition

Chapter Five

Ghost Stories: Real or Not?

Who's "The Brown Lady" ghost? What's the Bell Witch haunting? What happened at Moundsville jail?

Lady Dorothy Townshend lived in Raynham Hall. This is in England. She lived there in the 1700s. She cheated on her husband. Her husband locked her in the house. She died. Her ghost haunts the oak staircase.

Many people saw her ghost. King George IV stayed at Raynham. He saw her ghost. It was wearing a brown dress. It had a glowing face. Its eyes were carved out. It was standing beside his bed. Captain Provand and Indre Shira took a photo. This happened in 1936. The photo made "The Brown Lady" ghost famous.

This is one of the most famous haunted houses.

Real-World Connection

There's a ghost called "the Black-Eyed Child." It has black pits instead of eyes. It lives in England. Many people have seen it. Lee Brickley is hunting the ghost. His aunt first saw the ghost in 1982. She heard it cry for help. She saw black eyes. She was scared. Some believe the ghost is linked to a Celtic tribe. The tribe is known for making blood sacrifices. Others believe people are imagining the ghost. Brickley conducted many interviews. Witnesses say the child giggles or calls for help. This means it's trying to trap victims. It's leading people to danger. Brickley said, "In my opinion, the black-eyed child seems to be some kind of demon."

The Bell Witch haunting is famous. John Bell owned a farm. He lived in Tennessee. His family was haunted in the early 1800s. Bell kept seeing ghost animals. He heard scratching. He heard knocking. A ghost witch started haunting the Bells. It talked. It shook the house. It threw things. It attacked his daughter, Betsy. It pulled hair. It slapped. It pinched. It stuck pins. This continued for years.

Some people believe the Bell Witch was Kate Batts's ghost. Batts was Bell's neighbor. Bell cheated her out of land. Batts died. She swore she'd haunt Bell and his family.

President Andrew Jackson is believed to have investigated the Bell Witch haunting.

There's a jail in Moundsville, West Virginia. It was open for over 100 years. It housed 1,000 violent criminals. There were many fights. There were many deaths. The jail closed in 1995. But people think ghosts live there.

Guards saw dead prisoners walking around. Shadow Man is its most famous ghost. It lurks in shadows. Some people think it's a former guard. Others think it's a prisoner trying to escape. People hear ghosts fighting. They hear whispering. They feel cold spots.

Prisons and asylums are often haunted.

Did You Know?

- Winston Churchill visited the White House. He saw Abraham Lincoln's ghost.

- The Ghost Club was formed in 1862. It started in London. It studies ghosts. It exposes people who pretend to see ghosts.

- Ghosts can smell well. They like the smell of lemons.

- Cell phones have been killing off ghosts. Ghost sightings have dropped. Ghosts don't like the electronic noise made by phones.

- Dr. Hans Holzer came up with the term *ghost hunter*. He investigated a haunted house in Amityville. It's in New York. It was built on an Indian graveyard. The family was haunted.

- Common places to find ghosts are cemeteries, battlefields, churches, historic buildings, theaters, hotels, former navy ships, crime scenes, and abandoned hospitals or prisons.

- Al Capone was a famous mobster. His ghost appears when there are disrespectful visitors at his grave.

- Living ghosts are souls leaving the body of the still living.

- Ghosts are powerful around mirrors. They're especially strong when two mirrors are facing each other. This creates reflections of reflections. It makes a tunnel of light in the glass.

Consider This!

Take a Position: Many people have reported ghost sightings. Are ghosts real? Or are ghosts make-believe? Or both? What do you think? Argue your point with reasons and evidence.

Say What? Read the 45th Parallel Press book about Bloody Mary. Is Bloody Mary a ghost or something else? Explain how ghosts and Bloody Mary are similar. Explain how they are different.

Think About It! Read the 45th Parallel Press book about ghost hunters. Write a story about a ghost. Tell it from the ghost's perspective. Then, tell it from a ghost hunter's perspective.

Learn More

- Axelrod-Contrada, Joan. *The World's Most Famous Ghosts*. Mankato, MN: Capstone Press, 2012.
- Felix, Rebecca. *Ghosts: The Truth Behind History's Spookiest Spirits*. North Mankato, MN: Capstone Press, 2016.
- Hamilton, S. L. *Xtreme Monsters: Ghosts*. Edina, MN: ABDO and Daughters, 2010.
- Owen, Ruth. *Ghosts and Other Spirits of the Dead*. New York: Bearport Publishing, 2013.

Glossary

bound (BOUND) stuck, tied to

crisis (KRYE-sis) emergency

exorcism (EKS-or-siz-uhm) special religious ritual to rid people of devils or ghosts who have taken possession of their bodies

guardians (GAHR-dee-uhnz) protectors

haunt (HAWNT) to bother

intelligent (in-TEL-ih-juhnt) smart

invisible (in-VIZ-ih-buhl) not being seen

mediums (MEE-dee-uhmz) people who speak to ghosts

mists (MISTS) fogs

orbs (ORBZ) round balls of light

portals (POR-tuhlz) doorways of energy where spirits may enter or exit a location

pyramids (PIR-uh-midz) buildings shaped like a triangle used as tombs for Egyptian kings and queens

residual (rih-ZIJ-oo-uhl) leftover

souls (SOHLZ) spirits

summon (SUHM-uhn) to call

vengeful (VENJ-ful) full of revenge, wanting to get even

victims (VIK-tuhmz) people being haunted

vortexes (VOR-teks-iz) swirling lights

wail (WAYL) loud cry

Index

About the Author

Dr. Virginia Loh-Hagan is an author, university professor, former classroom teacher, and curriculum designer. She believes in ghosts. She lives in San Diego with her very tall husband and very naughty dogs. To learn more about her, visit www.virginialoh.com.